DATE DUE

Exploring British Values

Respect and Tolerance

Catherine Chambers

raintree
a Capstone company — publishers for children

Raintree is an imprint of Capstone Global Library Limited, a company incorporated in England and Wales having its registered office at 264 Banbury Road, Oxford, OX2 7DY – Registered company number: 6695582

www.raintree.co.uk
myorders@raintree.co.uk

Text © Capstone Global Library Limited 2018

The moral rights of the proprietor have been asserted.

Edited by Linda Staniford
Designed by Terri Poburka
Picture research by Pam Mitsakos
Original illustrations © Capstone Global Library Limited 2018
Illustrated by Graham Ross
Production by Steve Walker
Originated by Capstone Global Library
Printed and bound in China

ISBN 978 1 474 74079 1
21 20 19 18 17
10 9 8 7 6 5 4 3 2 1

British Library Cataloguing in Publication Data
A full catalogue record for this book is available from the British Library.

Acknowledgements
We would like to thank the following for permission to reproduce photographs: Alamy: BRIAN ANTHONY, 21, Colin Underhill, 17, Photofusion Picture Library, 25, Stephen Barnes, 19; Getty Images: Gideon Mendel/Corbis, 15, Hulton Deutsch/Corbis, 11; iStockphoto: funky-data, 5, kali9, 12; Newscom: KEYSTONE Pictures USA/ZUMAPRESS, 23, Lannis Waters/ZUMA Press, 27; North Wind Picture Archives: 7; Shutterstock: Attitude, design element, David Fowler, 29, Ermine, design element, John Gomez, 9, Lifestyle_Studio, design element, Sarunyu_foto, design element, URRRA, design element, wavebreakmedia, cover bottom

We would like to thank Marguerite Heath, Programmes Director at the Citizenship Foundation, for her invaluable help in the preparation of this book.

Every effort has been made to contact copyright holders of material reproduced in this book. Any omissions will be rectified in subsequent printings if notice is given to the publisher.

All the internet addresses (URLs) given in this book were valid at the time of going to press. However, due to the dynamic nature of the Internet, some addresses may have changed, or sites may have changed or ceased to exist since publication. While the author and publisher regret any inconvenience this may cause readers, no responsibility for any such changes can be accepted by either the author or the publisher.

Contents

Some words are shown in bold, **like this**. You can find out what they mean by looking in the glossary.

What are respect and tolerance?

Respect and **tolerance** make up one of the four key British values. These values help people to understand how to behave.

Respect means valuing all human beings. Tolerance means accepting the differences between people. Respect and tolerance together mean that we should treat people equally and without **discrimination**.

Respect and tolerance are an opportunity

Respect and tolerance help us understand our neighbours and our friends, whatever their backgrounds. They help us accept new neighbours from all regions of the British Isles and from different countries. They encourage us to treat all people the same, wherever they come from, however old they are and whatever their ability.

If a person shows a lack of respect or intolerance towards another, it is the fault of that person. It is not because they are a different colour, faith or race.

The Task Team investigates

Amina, Emily and Kwame are the Task Team. They report on school and community issues for their class. This time, the team investigates respect and tolerance through a local incident.

Teachers, governors and your own School Council want to make ALL items of school uniform COMPULSORY!

QUIETLY now please – I'm still speaking!

But Sir! Some of the uniform's old-fashioned and HORRIBLE!

Respect and tolerance are values that create peace and harmony within our homes, schools and communities. Everyone should be treated with respect and tolerance in their community and when they travel around Britain. These values also encourage us to learn about each other and the world around us.

Fact FILE

British values mean the values of the United Kingdom of England, Wales, Scotland and Northern Ireland. Many other countries have similar values. British laws support respect and tolerance. From the age of ten, we can be taken to court for breaking laws.

Young people from different backgrounds are enjoying an event in Britain.

EXACTLY! That's why the School Council and parents will help decide a NEW design.

Hmmm.

Yeah, right!

I bet the Head Teacher's already decided!

Respect and tolerance in our history

Britain was once a cluster of empty islands. Then, many people began to arrive from different countries in Europe. They did not always **respect** or tolerate each other. But over time, the values of respect and **tolerance** took shape and became part of British culture and law.

No respect for the poor

Hundreds of years ago, many of Britain's kings, queens and nobles did not respect the poor. The poor were peasants, who made up about 85 per cent of the population. They were made to work hard on rented farmland. They paid taxes and served in the Royal army when there was a war.

Fact FILE

King John I of England showed no respect for his subjects. But in 1215 his **barons** forced him to sign a document called Magna Carta. This was the start of laws that guaranteed respect for all people.

Invaders and abuse

William the Conqueror was a **Norman** king from France. He invaded England in 1066. William's laws made peasants' lives very difficult. He also showed no respect for Anglo-Saxon leaders in England's towns and villages. He replaced them all with Normans.

Faith and abuse

After 1066, people of the **Jewish** faith came to Britain. But they often suffered terrible hatred, **intolerance** and **prejudice** in a country where most people were **Catholic** Christians. In 1290, King Edward I of England **banished** all Jews from the country. They were not allowed to return until 1656, over 350 years later.

Medieval peasants worked hard on the land while powerful people lived in castles.

Weeell.... It's complicated, isn't it? LOTS of opinions.

EXACTLY! That's why you'll all be perfect!

I think he's dumped this one on us!

Yeah. It's what my Grandma calls "a hot potato"!

Magna Carta contained the first written laws on equality and respect. Since then, many other laws have been introduced. They have improved **equality**, respect and tolerance in all Britain's nations.

The Equality Act of 2010 contains the latest laws. The Act legally protects people from **discrimination** in the workplace and in wider society. The Act lists the different ways in which people could be discriminated against. These include a person's ethnic background, faith, age, disability or **gender**.

Testing respect and tolerance

Sometimes we find it hard to respect and tolerate people, even our friends. We might not understand a person's background or the way they live. This might make us judge someone harshly. So we have to try harder to see things from their point of view. This helps prevent hurt and arguments, or **conflict**.

When tolerance breaks

Respect and tolerance are tested in our school, community and country. Sometimes, certain **behaviours** and attitudes lead to conflict, or even violence. Our values have been tested over the centuries throughout Britain. They still are.

It helps to look back in history at examples of prejudice to increase our own sense of equality. Some examples of intolerance and disrespect puzzle us now. We do not understand why a particular group of people suffered prejudice. But we can understand why those who suffered became angry and afraid.

Protestors want Britain to continue its tradition of welcoming refugees.

Find out about an issue that has caused prejudice and conflict in Britain or your community. Learn the arguments on both sides. Does knowledge help you understand the conflict and the people involved?

9

The suffragettes

Over 100 years ago, women were not treated the same as men. So a group of women decided to fight for women's equality, respect and tolerance. These women were known as the suffragettes. They were especially angry that women could not vote in elections to choose Britain's government. So suffragettes rioted and chained themselves to railings. In 1908, 60,000 of them gathered outside Parliament in protest.

Now, our values are different. It is obvious to us that men and women should be respected and treated equally.

Power, respect and tolerance

The people who hold power make laws and set values for a whole nation. But these powerful people can also use the **media** to persuade people to think the same as they do. This is what happened with the suffragettes. By the end of World War I many politicians were in favour of women having the vote. The government eventually passed a law that allowed women to vote.

All over the world

We can increase our own respect and tolerance by studying the history of values and conflicts in other countries.

During World War II (1939–1945), Nazi Germany's leaders showed no respect for neighbouring countries. They even persecuted groups of people who had lived in Germany for generations. So after the war, the **United Nations (UN)** was set up to challenge lack of respect and tolerance in the world. The UN works to keep peace throughout the world, but it cannot prevent all conflict. Wars are still fought because of intolerance and disrespect.

Many suffragettes were imprisoned for protesting like this.

The UN was created on 24 October 1945. It supports respect and tolerance through its Universal Declaration of Human Rights. United Nations Day is celebrated on 24 October every year.

Words matter

It is against the law to show **intolerance** through physical violence. But how we use language is important, too. We can show **respect** and **tolerance** through thoughtful words or respectful silence.

When we use social media sites on our mobile phones or other electronic devices, we must still remember to treat others with respect.

Making mistakes

We all make mistakes. Sometimes we say something that seems to show a lack of respect and tolerance without meaning to. It is simply that we do not understand what hurts a person, and the reasons behind this.

This is why it is important to listen carefully to people. It helps us to find out about them. Listening also stops us judging people by their background or the way they look. It makes sure that we include people. Ignoring or shunning them shows a lack of respect and tolerance.

Gossip and lies

Respect and tolerance mean that we do not try to harm others by spreading gossip and lies about people. Social media has made this easy to do and difficult to undo. This is because it is hard to remove anything that has been written or spoken.

Get INVOLVED!

Draw up a code of conduct to show how your group, class or club members can listen and speak to each other respectfully. You could consider "thinking before speaking" as a starting point.

If we spread lies about people we are breaking **defamation** laws. Defamation means trying to destroy a person's good name by spreading lies about them. One type of defamation is **slander**, when lies are spread through spoken words. The other is **libel**, when lies are spread through written words.

What we look like

We show **respect** and **tolerance** by accepting the way people look. British values and the law tell us that we cannot **discriminate** against someone because of their skin colour, make-up, tattoos, hair, hairstyles or dress.

Dress and distress

Our dress can show our style and our culture. It can also show whether we are rich or poor, and our age. Sometimes there is a lack of respect for people who cannot afford to follow fashion or do not wish to. People are sometimes criticised if they have an unusual style, too.

Writing upsetting comments on social media is called **trolling**. Trolling can be very cruel and can spread widely. It does not stop at what people wear but also sometimes targets a person's skin colour, shape and size. This goes against British values of respect and tolerance.

Get INVOLVED!

Get together with others to create a slogan or rap rhyme that shows respect for each other's appearance.

14

Dress codes for work

There are often different dress codes for men and women at work. In some workplaces, women are expected to wear high-heeled shoes, which can harm feet. Many people believe this does not respect women's rights to safety and comfort.

In May 2016 a woman was told to leave her job because she refused to wear high heels. This goes against advice given in the 2010 Equality Act. So in 2017 a government committee called High Heels and Workplace Dress Codes published a report. It recommended that new laws should be made.

School uniforms mean that everyone wears the same clothes, regardless of their background.

How we speak

Our **accents** when we speak can tell people where we come from. Accents say nothing about our character or abilities. Yet the way we speak still makes people judge us. This is called **stereotyping**. Stereotyping shows **intolerance** and lack of **respect**.

Most of us speak with a **regional** accent, which comes from the part of Britain in which we live. Regional accents are often wrongly linked to a person's intelligence and willingness to work hard. Speaking clearly is more important than accent.

Accent and wealth

TV newsreaders speak clearly, and usually with Received Pronunciation (RP), or Standard English. This is a **neutral** accent that formed in 19th-century public schools, where children of rich people were educated.

Political, military and industrial leaders spoke with this accent.

So a class of powerful people without a regional accent was created. It led to a lack of respect between those who spoke RP and those who did not. In recent times, regional accents have been heard more widely on television, radio and in Parliament. **Prejudice** against certain accents is decreasing.

English keeps changing

English is a mixture of languages. It includes words that have been borrowed from many other countries. Over time, the British people have changed how these borrowed words are pronounced.

Borrowed words have enriched the English language. Knowing this, we can show respect and tolerance towards new words and accents that we might hear in our communities.

These shops display names from many countries.

You should explain your great drawings to the School Council, Finn.

Well... I dunno. I'm too new to present my ideas to the School Council. My accent's Glaswegian, and....

THAT won't be a problem!

Respecting beliefs

Some of us are brought up with a religious faith, while others are not. **Respecting** believers and non-believers alike is a British value. Not tolerating someone else's religious beliefs shows a lack of knowledge and understanding. It can also be against the law. People who follow a faith are also expected to follow British values and laws.

Faith in history

History shows us that Britain did not always follow just one faith. Britain's most ancient set of beliefs was based on worshipping the Sun as a creator and giver of life. Christianity came much later from the Middle East. It was brought by Roman invaders and Christian leaders over 2,000 years ago. Christianity became the faith of most people in Britain.

Since then, people have come to Britain bringing many other faiths. These include Judaism, Islam, Hinduism, Sikhism and Buddhism. Some British people have welcomed people of other faiths, while others have not.

Get INVOLVED!

We are often interested in each other's beliefs but feel we cannot ask about them. A good way to start is to ask about the meaning of our different festivals and celebrations.

Dividing a nation

In Northern Ireland, two different types of Christianity are followed. One is Catholicism and the other is Protestantism. There have always been divisions and conflicts between some **Catholics** and **Protestants**. But these became much worse from the 1970s. Many Protestants and Catholics hated each other and many people were killed. This time was known as the Troubles. Northern Ireland is more peaceful now as people work to respect each other's beliefs and viewpoints.

"Peace Walls" divided Northern Ireland's Protestant and Catholic neighbourhoods.

So how should we pitch our ideas?

Yes, I've been thinking really hard about this.

How about: "Our uniform is modern. But it respects everyone's ideas."

Let's see what the School Council thinks!

Faith and dress

Some faiths, such as traditional Islam and Judaism, have dress codes. These include dressing **modestly**, which means that the body has to be well covered. Girls and women wear a headscarf to cover their hair.

There is a lot of discussion about wearing headscarves in the **media**. It is a British value to discuss issues such as this with respect and **tolerance**. Most schools and workplaces have found it easy to include the headscarf in uniforms and dress codes. This means that Muslim girls and women can fit in well without going against their faith.

Faith and food

Food from other faiths or cultures can seem strange at first. But enjoying food is something that can unite us. In most faiths, food is prepared and eaten according to special rules and customs.

The lunch box we bring to school or work can contain anything from sandwiches to patties, or rice and curry. It may show some things about our faith and cultural background. We can show interest in our food traditions rather than disrespect or **intolerance**.

Get INVOLVED!

Set up a food-tasting session with others. If you do not like something, remember you can say so in a respectful way. For example, "I do not normally have this flavour or texture in my food. I will try it again another time."

VAISAKHI

Everyone is welcomed at the Sikh and Hindu festival of Vaisakhi.

TAFF

I liked your comment, Finn.

Yes. You said. "Uniform makes us all more equal."

The Head Teacher's going to outline our ideas in a letter to the parents.

Mmmm. I'm NERVOUS!

Rich and poor

In Britain, we show **respect** and **tolerance** towards people whether they are rich or poor. We respect all types of work, and people who cannot find work, in line with our British values.

Respect for the workplace

Some people help to keep our streets clean and our parks neat and bright with plants. The police help to keep our homes and streets safe.

Some jobs keep us healthy, such as nursing or medicine. Jobs such as teaching and training educate us. Other types of work bring wealth to Britain. These include manufacturing food and goods, and banking.

Respecting those without work

By the end of 2016, nearly 32 million British people aged between 16 and 64 had jobs. Only 4.8 per cent did not have jobs. But for these people, life is hard.

In some parts of Britain it is difficult to find work. Sometimes workplaces close down and people lose their jobs. It is important that we try and show sympathy with their situation. We can also try and sympathise with people who cannot work, due to illness or disability, or who are carers for others. Through showing sympathy with their situation we are giving them respect.

During World War II (1939-1945), people worked long hours to keep Britain going.

YOU *Decide!*

Try to find out from older people about their working lives. Did they work long hours? Was the work harder because of less automation? Was working life more difficult in the past? You decide!

Well. COST is one of the most important things!

Quite right! I'll post a list of prices for the new items tomorrow.

Yes. Parents need to think about that BEFORE the meeting.

Respect for where we live

Some homes are large and built in wealthy communities. Others are small and built in poorer communities. There are people who have no homes at all. We can try to imagine all these living conditions and learn to respect people who experience them.

Homes on the road

Traditional travelling communities, such as **Roma**, have lived in Britain for over 500 years. Their way of life is often misunderstood and some people who live in houses do not respect it.

The government counts travellers' caravans twice a year. In the summer of 2016, there were 21,419 caravans and 85 per cent of them stopped or stayed for long periods at properly **regulated** caravan sites. Travellers prefer these sites but local councils do not provide enough of them. Most travellers work and pay rents and taxes for the sites.

Respecting those without a home

Homelessness can happen to anyone. Some people lose their job and cannot pay for their home. A shortage of homes leads to homelessness. The cost of keeping a home can be too high for people to stay in it.

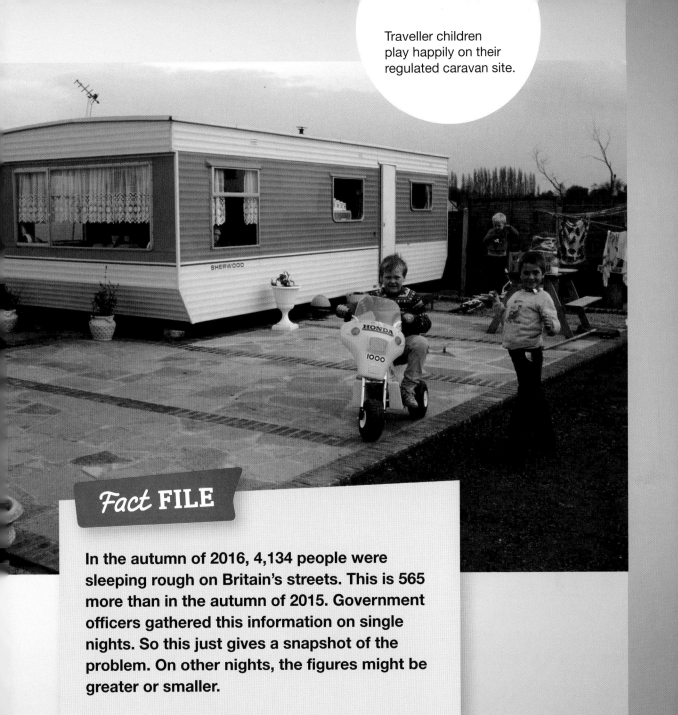

Traveller children play happily on their regulated caravan site.

Fact FILE

In the autumn of 2016, 4,134 people were sleeping rough on Britain's streets. This is 565 more than in the autumn of 2015. Government officers gathered this information on single nights. So this just gives a snapshot of the problem. On other nights, the figures might be greater or smaller.

There are other kids who can't stay long, too. For many reasons.

Yes. I'll sort out a special uniform budget to help them. BEFORE the meeting.

The meeting! SCARY!

Young and old

The relationship between young and older people is often a challenge. Each age group can find it hard to understand the other. This can be because their ways of life seem too different. **Respect** and **tolerance** can be reached if each age group listens to the other.

Older people are fascinating!

Housing, education, food, fashion, music and entertainment were all very different for older people. But you will probably find that feelings and relationships were very similar.

Television programmes such as *Strictly Come Dancing* and retro fashions have revived styles that older people will recognise. Now, many age groups enjoy them. These are things that we can all share.

Bringing age groups together

In the south-west of England, an art project called Paint Pals brings old and young people together. Schoolchildren and elderly people in care homes share ideas and memories through art. They send each other postcards and meet up to chat. The children help frailer, older people to paint and draw.

This female World War II pilot must have had fascinating stories to tell when she was older.

Get INVOLVED!

People in Britain live longer on average than they once did. This means we have a better chance of finding out about life in Britain a long time ago. In 1983, there were 322 people aged 90 or over out of 100,000.
By 2013 there were 822 people aged 90 or over out of 100,000.

EMILY!

But Grandma! Your ideas are so OLD!

YES NO EXTRA IDEAS

Hmmm. Thank you Emily. I do add internet research to my ancient wisdom!

NO EXTRA IDEAS

The future for respect and tolerance

Respect and tolerance are British values that lead to happy communities and a more peaceful world. They depend on us listening, thinking before speaking and mixing with people from all backgrounds.

Thinking for ourselves

The future of respect and tolerance in Britain depends partly on us thinking for ourselves. We hear false ideas about people all the time in the media. We can seek the truth through careful research, and make up our own minds – but this takes a lot of courage.

Challenges for British values

Britain has belonged to the European Union (EU) since 1975. The EU upholds values of respect and tolerance in its human rights laws. In June 2016, Britain voted to leave the EU in a **referendum**. The decision to leave is now known as Brexit (Britain's Exit). Britain will go back to having more of its own laws.

The vote led to a lot of arguments in families and communities. It led to lack of respect and tolerance for people with different ideas. **Racism** increased, especially towards people from EU countries.

Britain still belongs to the United Nations. Article 7 of the UN Declaration of Human Rights upholds equality and freedom from discrimination, which depend on respect and tolerance. As a UN member, Britain still has to follow these goals.

We can enjoy fun times together, and share the hard times.

And you have the right to say so. But you can put your scarf back on!

Glossary

accent the way people speak, that identifies where they are from

automation use of machines rather than people to do jobs, especially in factories

banish force someone to leave a place and never return

baron nobleman in medieval times

behaviour the way a person acts

Catholic relating to the Roman Catholic church; the religion followed in Britain until the 16th century

conflict strong disagreement

defamation trying to destroy someone's good reputation by spreading lies about them

discrimination unfair behaviour to others based on such things as their age, ethnic background or gender

equality the same rights for everyone

gender male or female identity

intolerance lack of tolerance; unwillingness to learn about other people's beliefs, ideas or actions

Jewish following the religion and cultural traditions of the Jews, the ancient Hebrew tribes of Israel

libel false statements that are written or printed

media means of mass communication, such as newspapers, radio, TV and the Internet

modest decent, not showy

Norman one of the peoples originally from Scandinavia who invaded Northern France in the 10th century; the Normans conquered England in 1066

neutral having no distinctive type or characteristics

prejudice hatred or unfair treatment people who belong to a certain socia group, such as an ethnic background or religion

Protestant relating to the branch of Christianity that broke off from the Catholic church in the 16th century

racism treating people unkindly and unfairly because they are from a different ethnic background

referendum public vote to decide a question

regional relating to a particular area a country

regulate control or manage accordir to laws

respect accept someone's difference and their equal rights

Roma another name for the Romani or gypsy people, who tend not to m with the rest of society; they have been persecuted throughout history

slander false statements that are spoken

stereotype hold a simplified idea or opinion of a person or group of peo

tolerance acceptance of people's beliefs or actions that differ from ou own beliefs or actions

trolling writing comments on social media that are intended to anger or upset people

United Nations (UN) international organization formed to keep peace the world and to defend human rig

Find out more

Books

You might like to look at these other books on British Values:

Let's Vote on it! (British Values), Christopher Yeates (Gresham Books, 2016)

Looking After Britain (British Values), Christopher Yeates (Gresham Books, 2016)

Our Country, Our World (British Values), Christopher Yeates (Gresham Books, 2016)

What Does It Mean to be British?, Nick Hunter (Raintree, 2017)

Websites

www.bbc.co.uk/newsround
The CBBC Newsround website gives lots of interesting features on rights and values around the world.

www.un.org/en/universal-declaration-human-rights/
On this site you can read the United Nations Declaration of Human Rights.

www.unesco.org/new/en/social-and-human-sciences/themes/ fight-against-discrimination/promoting-tolerance/
This site explains the United Nation's ideas on respect and tolerance.

Index